South Korea

ANITA YASUDA

www.av2books.com

MEDIA ENHANCED BOOKS
AV² BY WEIGL™
ADDED VALUE • AUDIO VISUAL

AV² provides enriched content that supplements and complements this book. Weigl's AV² books strive to create inspired learning and engage young minds in a total learning experience.

Your AV² Media Enhanced books come alive with...

Audio
Listen to sections of the book read aloud.

Key Words
Study vocabulary, and complete a matching word activity.

Video
Watch informative video clips.

Quizzes
Test your knowledge.

Go to www.av2books.com, and enter this book's unique code.

Embedded Weblinks
Gain additional information for research.

Slide Show
View images and captions, and prepare a presentation.

BOOK CODE

S 2 9 4 5 6 9

AV² by Weigl brings you media enhanced books that support active learning.

Try This!
Complete activities and hands-on experiments.

... and much, much more!

Published by AV² by Weigl
350 5th Avenue, 59th Floor
New York, NY 10118
Websites: www.av2books.com   www.weigl.com

Library of Congress Cataloging-in-Publication Data

Yasuda, Anita.
  South Korea / Anita Yasuda.
     pages cm. — (Exploring countries)
  Includes bibliographical references and index.
  ISBN 978-1-4896-3066-7 (hard cover : alk. paper) — ISBN 978-1-4896-3067-4 (soft cover : alk. paper) — ISBN 978-1-4896-3068-1 (single user ebook)
  — ISBN 978-1-4896-3069-8 (multi-user ebook)
  1. Korea (South)—Juvenile literature. 2. Korea (South)—Description and travel—Juvenile literature. I. Title.
  DS902.Y37 2014
  951.95—dc23   2014038998

Printed in the United States of America in Brainerd, Minnesota
1 2 3 4 5 6 7 8 9 19 18 17 16 15

012015
WEP160115

Project Coordinator Heather Kissock
Art Director Terry Paulhus

Photo Credits
Every reasonable effort has been made to trace ownership and to obtain permission to reprint copyright material. The publishers would be pleased to have any errors or omissions brought to their attention so that they may be corrected in subsequent printings.

Weigl acknowledges Getty Images as its primary image supplier for this title. Page 4 photo © UTATHYA BHADRA PHOTOGRAPHY.

Contents

AV² Book Code 2

South Korea Overview 4

Exploring South Korea 6

Land and Climate 8

Plants and Animals 10

Natural Resources 11

Tourism 12

Industry 14

Goods and Services 15

Indigenous Peoples 16

Early Rulers 17

The Age of Dynasties 18

Population 20

Politics and Government 21

Cultural Groups 22

Arts and Entertainment 24

Sports 26

Mapping South Korea 28

Quiz Time 30

Key Words 31

Index 31

Log on to www.av2books.com 32

South Korea Overview

South Korea is located on the southern half of the Korean **peninsula** on the continent of Asia. The country also includes more than 3,000 small offshore islands. Its official name is the **Republic** of Korea. The northern portion of the peninsula belongs to North Korea, or the Democratic People's Republic. Until the mid-20th century, the two Koreas were united. South Korea is known for its rich culture and history, as well as the artistic and technological skills of its people. The rugged land is covered with mountains. South Korea's **economy** is one of the strongest in Asia. Many citizens have a high **standard of living**.

The city of Jinhae hosts South Korea's largest cherry blossom festival.

South Koreans celebrate National Liberation Day on August 15. On that day in 1945, Korea was no longer under Japanese rule.

Kimchi is a traditional cabbage dish eaten at almost every meal in South Korea.

South Koreans honor the birth of spiritual leader Gautama Buddha with lotus lanterns.

Changdeokgung Palace, built in the 15th century, has gardens with a colorful pavilion.

Exploring South Korea

South Korea covers a total area of 38,502 square miles (99,720 square kilometers). It stretches 600 miles (970 km) from north to south and 135 miles (220 km) from east to west. South Korea's only land border is with North Korea. South Korea touches two major bodies of water. The Sea of Japan, also called the East Sea, is to the east, and the Yellow Sea is to the west. The Korea Strait is a narrow body of water that separates southern Korea from southwestern Japan.

Seoul

China

N

Jeju Island

Map Legend

South Korea

Land

Water

Nakdong River

Jeju Island

▲ Mount Jiri

📍 Capital City

SCALE

25 Miles

25 Kilometers

Jeju Island

South Korea's southernmost island is called Jeju. Jeju Island features the tallest mountain in the country, Mount Halla. The mountain, now an inactive volcano, is 6,398 feet (1,950 meters) high.

North Korea

Nakdong River

Seoul

SOUTH KOREA

Yellow Sea

Sea of Japan (East Sea)

Mount Jiri

Korea Strait

Jeju Island

Mount Jiri

Japan

Seoul

Seoul became the capital of South Korea in 1948. It was formerly the capital of Korea. The largest city in the country, Seoul offers historic palaces and temples, open-air food markets, and modern shopping centers.

Mount Jiri

Mount Jiri measures 6,283 feet (1,915 m) high. It is the tallest peak on the South Korean mainland. Mount Jiri is part of South Korea's first national park of the same name, which was founded in 1967.

Nakdong River

The Nakdong River measures 325 miles (525 km) long. It is South Korea's longest river. The Nakdong flows from north to south and then enters a **delta** region known for its agricultural land.

LAND AND CLIMATE

Mountains and highlands cover more than 70 percent of South Korea. There are two major mountain ranges. The Taebaek range runs north to south along Korea's eastern coast. The Sobaek Mountains run across the center of southern South Korea.

From these ranges flow South Korea's largest rivers. They are the Han, Geumg, and Yeong, as well as the Nakdong. The Han River begins in the Taebaek Mountains before flowing through Seoul. The Nakdong River also starts in the Taebaek range. Both the Yeong and Geumg Rivers begin in the Sobaek Mountains. They travel through southwestern South Korea to the Yellow Sea.

Snowfall is heaviest in northern South Korea, including Seoul.

South Korea's western regions are covered in flat lands called plains. The Southwestern Plain extends across the western half of the peninsula. It has rolling hills and plains. The Southern Plain is found along the south coast.

South Korea has the four seasons of spring, summer, fall, and winter. In the spring, seasonal winds from China send thick clouds of yellow dust into Korea. The dust is sand from the Gobi Desert. By mid-April, warmer weather arrives, and cherry blossoms begin to bloom.

In the summer, a wind called the Asian **monsoon** brings warm moist air from the Pacific Ocean. South Korean summers are hot and humid. The country also experiences **typhoons** at this time of year. These storms bring heavy rain and strong winds that can cause damage. Autumn is cool and dry. South Korean winters are snowy and cold.

The Seomjin River starts in Mount Jiri, stretches 132 miles (212 km), and empties into the Korea Strait.

PLANTS AND ANIMALS

South Korea has more than 100,000 plant and animal **species**. Forests of spruce and pine are common in the north. The mountain area of Uljin is known for its diamond pine trees. One of the region's longest-living pines is 500 years old. Broadleaved oak trees grow in central South Korea.

South Korea's forests are home to many small animals, including badgers and weasels. Larger animals such as bears and lynx have become rare. This is because much of their natural habitat has been lost due to human activities. Asiatic black bears are sometimes seen in northern mountains and the area between the two Koreas called the demilitarization zone (DMZ).

The DMZ is 160 miles (250 km) long and about 2.5 miles (4 km) wide. Human access to this area is controlled. As a result, it has filled with animals living in nature. Wild boar, water deer, and the rare long-tailed goral all find shelter there.

The red-crowned crane lives in South Korea's coastal areas. It is one of the rarest birds in the world.

More Than
100
Number of fish species in South Korea.

8 OUNCES
Weight of a newborn Asiatic black bear. (227 grams)

1,100 Years
Age of the oldest ginkgo tree in South Korea.

About 500
Number of bird species in South Korea.

NATURAL RESOURCES

South Korea does not have a great deal of natural resources. For many of these resources, the country relies on imports, or goods brought in from other areas. For example, almost 70 percent of South Korea's food comes from other places. The country's fertile land is located near rivers. The soil there is good for growing Chinese cabbage, soybeans, rice, and other crops. South Korea's citrus crops are grown on Jeju. Its warm climate and rich soil help farmers produce oranges, grapefruit, pears, and pineapples.

Fish and shellfish are an important food source. Freshwater eels, catfish, and carp are caught in lakes. Trout are found in mountain streams. Nationwide, more than 3.6 million tons (3.3 million metric tons) of fish, including anchovy, mackerel, and squid, are caught each year.

Although South Korea has limited mineral resources, there are deposits of coal, graphite, and lead. The country's largest coalfield is in Samcheok. The country also uses hydropower, or the energy of moving water, to produce electricity. Today, the Han River is used to produce energy in this way, though it provides only 2 percent of South Korea's electricity. In the past, most of South Korea's forests were cut down for fuel. Today, the national government supports efforts to plant trees.

4 Million
Number of tons of rice that are harvested in South Korea per year. (3.6 million metric tons)

ALMOST 7%
Portion of the labor force working in agriculture.

1 Million
Number of visitors to Hwacheon's annual Mountain Trout Ice Festival.

Busan in southeastern South Korea is the center of the fish and seafood industry.

TOURISM

South Korea attracts 12 million visitors from around the world each year. People come to see ancient palaces and temples, traditional villages, and local festivals. They also come to hike and ski.

Lotte World Adventure in Seoul is the world's largest indoor theme park.

More than 10 million tourists visit Seoul each year. The city is known for its mix of modern skyscrapers, historic sites, and shopping. Myeongdong, north of the Han River, is one of the most popular shopping districts. Besides having stores that sell high-priced items, the area has streets lined with food stalls offering traditional Korean delicacies. These include eomuk, a deep-fried minced-fish treat. Nearby, visitors flock to the country's oldest traditional market, Namdaemun.

Next to the market is a 14th-century gate, which is also called Namdaemun. The gate once was part of a wall surrounding Seoul. After burning almost to the ground in 2008, the gate and a wooden **pagoda** were rebuilt in 2013.

The National Museum of Korea in Seoul receives more than 3 million visitors a year.

There are many other historic sites in Seoul. People visit the president's residence, called the Blue House. From there, it is a quick walk on Seoul's main boulevard, Sejongno, to the palace of Gyeongbokgung. Within the palace grounds is the National Palace Museum of Korea, which displays about 15,000 artworks from all periods of Korean history. The National Folk Museum of Korea is also within the palace grounds. Nearby is Bukchon Hanok Village. A hanok is a traditional Korean home.

Outside of Seoul, there is more to see and do. People take in the scenery at national parks, such as Seoraksan National Park in the country's mountainous northeast. Many people travel to the island of Jeju to hike Mount Halla.

At the first sign of snow, skiers and snowboarders flock to the slopes of Yongpyong. With 31 slopes, it is the biggest ski resort in South Korea. When the country hosts the 2018 Winter Olympics, athletes will compete at Yongpyong.

Tourism BY THE NUMBERS

ABOUT 900
Number of traditional Korean homes in Bukchon Hanok Village.

113,000 Number of items in the collection of the National Folk Museum of Korea.

150,000 Number of roof tiles on the Blue House.

The Phoenix Park ski resort is only two hours away from Seoul by car.

INDUSTRY

Almost one-fourth of South Korean workers are employed in manufacturing. The shipbuilding, automotive, and electronics industries have helped make South Korea's economy the fourth-largest in Asia, after China, India, and Japan. The two largest vehicle manufacturers are Hyundai Motor Company and Kia Motors Corporation. Hyundai's Ulsan factory is the largest single factory in the world. It employs more than 34,000 people and is capable of producing 1.5 million cars per year.

South Korea is also a leading manufacturer of electronics products. Samsung Electronics is one of the world's biggest technology companies. Workers make memory chips, smartphones, and televisions.

Hyundai Heavy Industries is the largest shipbuilder in the world. It produces many types of ships, including tankers, car carriers, and submarines. The company has 15 percent of the world's shipbuilding market. Its shipyard stretches for more than 2 miles (3 km) along the coast of Mipo Bay in the southeast.

54%
Portion of the South Korean economy that comes from selling goods to other countries.

123,000 Number of people employed by Samsung Electronics globally.

25.9 Million Number of workers in South Korea.

Every year, South Korea produces more than 4 million cars, many of which are exported, or sold to other countries.

GOODS AND SERVICES

More than two-thirds of the South Korean labor force works in service industries. These industries provide services to people instead of producing goods. Examples of service workers include government officials, teachers, lawyers, engineers, hotel and restaurant workers, and airline flight crews.

As a member of the 21-nation group Asia-Pacific Economic Cooperation (APEC), South Korea trades easily with other APEC countries. There are almost no tariffs, or taxes, on goods brought into one APEC country from another. South Korea's top-three trade partners, China, the United States, and Japan, are APEC members.

In 2011, South Korea signed a free trade agreement with the European Union (EU), an economic and political organization of 28 countries. This kind of agreement removes barriers such as taxes to improve the flow of goods between countries. The EU is now South Korea's 10th-largest trading partner.

South Korea's top exports are electrical and electronic equipment, vehicles, ships, and machinery. South Korea has 16 ports, a large network of roads, 1,800 miles (3,000 km) of railroads, and 111 airports to help transport goods. Busan has the country's largest port.

More than 20,000 flight attendants, pilots, and ground staff work for Korean Air, the country's largest airline.

Goods and Services BY THE NUMBERS

2004

Year high-speed rail travel began in South Korea, connecting Seoul and Busan.

23%
Portion of South Korea's exports that are sold to China.

$560 Billion
Value of South Korea's exports in 2013.

INDIGENOUS PEOPLES

People may have begun living on the Korean peninsula as long as 500,000 years ago. **Prehistoric** stone tools have been found near the city of Gongju, which is south of Seoul. Between 7000 and 3000 BC, tribes arrived from Mongolia and Manchuria, a region that is now part of China. Other groups moved into Korea from Siberia, which now makes up most of eastern Russia.

The people fished, hunted, and gathered plants for food. Later, they planted grains, made pottery, and lived in walled towns. They also built huge stone tombs called dolmens throughout the region.

Korean legend says an ancient ruler named Dangun established the first Korean **kingdom** in 2333 BC. Dangun named his kingdom Gojoseon, which means "land of morning calm." The capital of Gojoseon was on the site of the modern-day city of Pyongyang, North Korea's capital.

Amsa-dong Prehistoric Settlement Site in Seoul recreates Korean life from more than 6,000 years ago. On display are huts with fire pits and grass roofs.

EARLY RULERS

In 108 BC, Chinese emperor, or ruler, Wudi of the Han **Dynasty** invaded and took control of the Korean peninsula. The Han set up four districts to control the region. In one of them, Lolang, Chinese rule lasted for 400 years. The Chinese introduced their writing system to Korea, as well as the practice of growing rice. They also brought other aspects of their culture, including the religions **Buddhism** and **Confucianism**.

About 300 AD, the Han Dynasty began to collapse. Korean tribes united and formed their own kingdoms. The Goguryeo kingdom held the northern half of the Korean peninsula, as well as northeast China. Farther south were the kingdoms of Silla to the east and Baekje to the west.

By 668 AD, Silla was able to defeat the Goguryeo and Baekje kingdoms, uniting the Korean peninsula. At this time, astronomy, music, and metal work flourished. Silla sent **monks** to China to study **architecture** and literature. Rulers gave land to peasants in exchange for a portion of their crops. The last Silla king was overthrown in the 10th century.

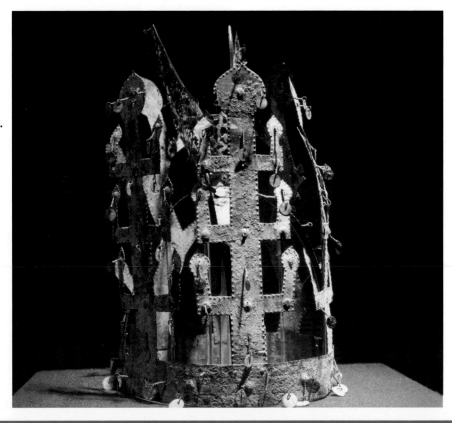

The rulers of Silla had bronze crowns originally covered with jewels.

THE AGE OF DYNASTIES

In 918 AD, the military general Wang Geon established the Goryeo Dynasty. Korea's name comes from this dynasty. The general's hometown of Kaeseong in present-day North Korea became the capital. By 936, the dynasty controlled all of Korea, but forces from Mongolia were often attacking. In 1231, Mongol ruler Kublai Khan succeeded in capturing Goryeo. However, in 1356, the Mongols were driven out.

Yi Song-gye, founder of the Joseon Dynasty, is buried in a royal tomb in the city of Guri near Seoul.

During the Goryeo Dynasty, which ended in 1392, Koreans built hundreds of Buddhist temples. Buddhist monks began carving more than 80,000 woodblocks with Buddhist writings, which today are housed at the Haeinsa Temple on Mount Gaya. When warlord Yi Song-gye overthrew the king in 1392, he named his dynasty Joseon after the earlier legendary Korean kingdom of Gojoseon. As king, Yi Song-gye moved his capital to present-day Seoul. He replaced the state religion of Buddhism with Confucianism.

The *Tripitaka Koreana*, a collection of Buddhist texts at the Haeinsa Temple, was engraved on woodblocks between 1237 and 1248.

For more than 500 years, 27 Joseon rulers led Korea. It was a time of many advances in art and science. In 1446, during the reign of King Sejong, the Korean alphabet, called Hangul, was created. The alphabet was easy to write and learn. The king was a strong supporter of scholars. He encouraged research, including in the fields of astronomy and geography.

In the 16th century, Japan invaded the Korean peninsula several times. Backed by the Ming Dynasty of China, the Joseon rulers were able to fight off the Japanese troops. Korean admiral Yi Soon-shin's armored ships played an important role in victories at sea. Afterward, Korea closed its borders for nearly 200 years. It became known as the **Hermit** Kingdom.

In the mid-1800s, European countries and the United States demanded that Korea open its borders to trade. Later in the 19th century, the Joseon government became unpopular within the country. When an uprising began in 1894, troops from China and Japan came into Korea to help the government. Soon, these armies fought each other for control of Korea. In the end, Japan won. By 1910, Korea was a Japanese **colony**, and it remained under Japanese control until the end of World War II in 1945.

24 Letters in the Hangul alphabet.

362 Number of stones in Cheomseongdae, Asia's oldest tower for observing stars, built in Gyeongju during the 7th century.

About 20,000 Number of Buddhist temples in South Korea.

From the 15th to 19th centuries, the Korean navy used a type of warship called the *geobukseon*, or "turtle ship." The vessel's overlapping metal plates gave protection much like a turtle's shell.

POPULATION

South Korea has more than 49 million residents. It is a densely populated country, which means South Korea has a large number of people for its land area. The population is not evenly spread out over the land. Most South Koreans live in **urban** areas. Gyeonggi, which includes the city of Seoul, is the most populated **province** in the country. Almost half of all South Koreans live there.

The city of Seoul is home to more than 9.5 million people. The port city of Busan is the next-largest city, with more than 3 million residents. Incheon, a city near Seoul, has a population of 2.6 million people.

People born in other countries make up less than 3 percent of the South Korean population. Many of these people are workers seeking better job opportunities. Since 2000, the number of foreign workers in South Korea has risen. Most workers are from other Asian countries, including Vietnam and the Philippines.

26 Number of countries with larger populations than South Korea.

14% Portion of South Korea's population under the age of 15.

98% Portion of people age 15 and older who can read and write.

The city and surrounding region of Seoul has become one of the world's largest metropolitan areas.

POLITICS AND GOVERNMENT

After World War II, U.S. forces controlled the southern half of the Korean peninsula. This area became the independent country of South Korea in 1948. North Korea became a separate country the same year. In 1950, North Korea attacked South Korea. The Korean War lasted for three years. A truce ending the fighting was signed in 1953, and the DMZ was created.

South Korea's first president, Syngman Rhee, limited people's freedom. Protests by students and other Koreans in 1960 forced him to resign. Then, a series of military rulers controlled South Korea until 1981. The people's demands for democratic changes grew in the country. After Roh Tae-Woo was elected president in 1987, a new **constitution** was written giving people greater rights.

South Korea's president is elected for a five-year term and is allowed to serve only one term. The president chooses a prime minister, who is the head of the **cabinet**. The cabinet has between 15 and 30 members. The prime minister must be approved by the legislature, which is called the National Assembly. The National Assembly has one chamber with 300 members elected for four-year terms.

 19 Age a citizen of South Korea must be to vote in a national election.

 9 Number of provinces in South Korea.

2013
Year that Park Geun-hye, the first female president of South Korea, took office.

The South Korean legislature meets in the National Assembly Building in Seoul.

CULTURAL GROUPS

As a member of the National Assembly, Jasmine Lee has supported immigrant families in South Korea.

Most South Koreans share a similar background. Modern-day Koreans are descended from people who came from northern Asia in prehistoric times. South Korea's population does not include many people from a non-Korean **ethnic group**. The largest such group in South Korea is people of Chinese descent. In the 1880s, many people left northern China due to political unrest and settled in what is now South Korea.

With the arrival of more **immigrants** in recent years, some experts believe that, by 2020, one in five South Korean families will have members of non-Korean ethnic groups. One of the country's best-known immigrants is Jasmine Lee, who was born in the Philippines. In 2012, she became the first non-ethnic Korean elected to the National Assembly.

South Korea's official language is Korean. It is spoken throughout the country. The standard form of the language is the one spoken in Seoul. However, other **dialects** are spoken in some regions of the country. The dialect spoken on Jeju Island differs so greatly from standard Korean that **UNESCO** recognizes it as another language.

Chinese culture has influenced the Korean art of fine lettering, called calligraphy.

After South Korea hosted the Summer Olympics in 1988, the national government began to encourage English language education. English is now taught in many schools and spoken by a large number of South Koreans. The Ministry of Education hires some language teachers from English-speaking countries, such as Canada and the United States, to work in South Korean schools.

A number of religions are practiced in present-day South Korea. More than three out of ten South Koreans are Christians. About 24 percent are Protestant, and almost 8 percent are Roman Catholic. After Christianity, Buddhism is the next-largest religion, practiced by 24 percent of the population.

Park Geun-hye welcomed Pope Francis to South Korea in 2014. It was the first visit to South Korea in 25 years by a head of the Roman Catholic Church.

ARTS AND ENTERTAINMENT

Korean arts are thousands of years old. They have changed and grown through time. The South Korean Ministry of Culture, Sports, and Tourism supports and preserves traditional and modern literature, art, music, dance, and drama. UNESCO World Heritage Sites, museums, and theaters offer culture of all kinds.

Buddha is a common subject of various kinds of art in South Korea.

In the past, Korean decorative arts, such as **ceramics**, were inspired by nature. Designs featured blossoms, birds, and fish. Later, arts and architecture reflected Buddhism. When Confucianism gained in importance, there was a growth in arts such as landscape painting.

Korea has many kinds of traditional music and dance. Pansori is a kind of Korean musical drama in which a drummer accompanies a singer. Some Korean dances were traditionally performed at religious ceremonies. Court dances featured colorful costumes and slow rhythms.

Buchaechum is a Korean folk dance in which performers use colorful fans to look like blooming flowers, butterflies, or a sea wave.

In the late 1990s, South Korean entertainment began to grow in popularity around the world. This included pop music, films, and television shows. The trend was nicknamed *Hallyu,* meaning "Korean Wave."

Before the 1990s, few South Korean films were ever shown outside the country. From the 1990s on, this began to change. South Korean films have won awards at major film festivals in Cannes, France, and Venice, Italy.

South Korean TV dramas and pop music have been nicknamed K-Pop. Many Korean actors are stars outside their country. They include Bae Yong-jun, who starred in the hit TV drama *Winter Sonata*, and singer-actor Jeong Ji-hun, better known by his stage name Rain. In 2012, Psy's "Gangnam Style" topped the pop-music charts of best-selling songs.

2007 Year Jeon Do-yeon won the Best Actress Award at the Cannes film festival.

50% Portion of films shown in South Korea that are made there.

1996 First year of the Busan International Film Festival, now the biggest such festival in Asia.

In a *Time* magazine annual poll, readers voted pop star Rain the most influential person in the world three different years.

SPORTS

South Korea is known for the martial art of taekwondo. The sport is said to teach a person skills that will train the body and mind. Today, about 8 million people in more than 200 countries are taking part in taekwondo.

Another traditional sport in South Korea is ssireum, a form of wrestling. Each player grabs at a cloth tied around the opponent's waist and thigh. The object is to wrestle the opposing player to the ground. There are professional South Korean ssireum teams, and some matches are televised.

Hwang Kyung-seon of South Korea has won two Olympic gold medals in taekwondo.

Many South Koreans enjoy watching and participating in baseball, soccer, golf, swimming, and figure skating. Figure skater Yuna Kim won a gold medal in the ladies' singles competition at the 2010 Winter Olympics in Vancouver, Canada. She took home a silver medal at the 2014 Winter Games in Sochi, Russia.

One of South Korea's most popular sports for fans and players is soccer. South Korean soccer fans are called the Red Devils and wear red, as their national team does. The South Korean national team has qualified for more World Cup championship tournaments than any other team in Asia. In 2014, it qualified for the World Cup in Brazil.

In 2014, Yuna Kim retired from competitive skating and became an official ambassador for the 2018 Winter Games in South Korea.

South Korea has eight professional baseball teams. Some players have joined American major league teams. In 1994, pitcher Chan Ho Park became the first Korean-born athlete to play in Major League Baseball (MLB) when he signed a contract with the Los Angeles Dodgers. Today, several South Korean players, including outfielder Shin-soo Choo of the Texas Rangers, have contracts with MLB teams.

South Korea has hosted several international sporting events over the years. In the 1988 Summer Olympics, more than 160 countries and 13,000 athletes competed. The official theme of the games was "Peace, Harmony, and Progress." For the 2018 Winter Olympics in South Korea, Pyeongchang will be the official host city. The theme of these games will be "New Horizons."

1972 Year the World Taekwondo Federation was established.

12TH South Korea's rank in medals won at the 2014 Winter Olympics.

2008 Year the South Korean national baseball team won a gold medal at the Olympic Games in Beijing, China.

11 Number of Ladies Professional Golf Association tournament victories, through the end of 2013, for South Korean golfer Jiyai Shin.

In 2013, Hyun-Jin Ryu became the first South Korean pitcher to start a Major League postseason game.

Mapping South Korea

We use many tools to interpret maps and to understand the locations of features such as cities, states, lakes, and rivers. The map below has many tools to help interpret information on the map of South Korea.

Map of South Korea

MAP LEGEND

★ Capital City
● City
Body of Water

River
Country Border
▲ Mountains

Longitude & Latitude
South Korea
Other Countries

N
W   E
S

SCALE
0   80 Miles

0   80 Kilometers

Mapping Tools

- The compass rose shows north, south, east, and west. The points in between represent northeast, northwest, southeast, and southwest.
- The map scale shows that the distances on a map represent much longer distances in real life. If you measure the distance between objects on a map, you can use the map scale to calculate the actual distance in miles or kilometers between those two points.
- The lines of latitude and longitude are long lines that appear on maps. The lines of latitude run east to west and measure how far north or south of the equator a place is located. The lines of longitude run north to south and measure how far east or west of the Prime Meridian a place is located. A location on a map can be found by using the two numbers where latitude and longitude meet. This number is called a coordinate and is written using degrees and direction. For example, the city of Seoul would be found at 38°N and 127°E on a map.

Map It!

Using the map and the appropriate tools, complete the activities below.

Locating with latitude and longitude
1. Which body of water is located at 35°N and 125°E?
2. Which mountain is located at 33°N and 127°E?
3. Which city is found at 35°N and 129°E?

Distances between points
4. Using the map scale and a ruler, calculate the approximate distance between Seoul and Incheon.
5. Using the map scale and a ruler, calculate the approximate length of Jeju Island.
6. Using the map scale and a ruler, calculate the approximate distance between Seoul and Jeju Island.

Quiz Time

Test your knowledge of South Korea by answering these questions.

1 What is the capital of South Korea?

2 Which river flows through Seoul?

3 What company is the largest automobile manufacturer in South Korea?

4 Which island has a dialect that differs so greatly from standard Korean that it is recognized as another language?

5 What is the largest crop grown in South Korea?

6 When was Changdeokgung Palace built?

7 What portion of South Korea's workforce is employed in service industries?

8 What is the name of the first female president of South Korea?

9 Which martial art is South Korea known for?

10 What is the name of the host city for the 2018 Winter Olympics?

ANSWERS
1. Seoul
2. Han River
3. Hyundai
4. Jeju Island
5. Rice
6. 15th century
7. More than two-thirds
8. Park Geun-hye
9. Taekwondo
10. Pyeongchang

Key Words

architecture: the style in which buildings are designed

Buddhism: a religion that grew out of the teachings of Gautama Buddha more than 2,500 years ago

cabinet: a group of officials who give advice to a government leader

ceramics: objects made of clay heated to a very high temperature

colony: an area or country that is under the control of another country

Confucianism: the teachings of the Chinese philosopher Confucius

constitution: a written document stating a country's basic principles and laws

delta: an area of land that forms where a river separates into smaller rivers before flowing into the ocean

dialects: forms of a language that are spoken or known only in certain areas or by certain groups of people

dynasty: a series of rulers from the same family

economy: the wealth and resources of a country or area

ethnic group: a group of people who share the same cultural background

hermit: a person who lives alone and does not interact with other people

immigrants: people who move to a new country or area to live

kingdom: a territory ruled by a king or a queen

monks: men who belong to a religious order and follow its rules and ways of life

monsoon: a wind that blows at a certain time of year in parts of Asia and often brings heavy rain

pagoda: a Buddhist tower with several stories

peninsula: a piece of land surrounded on three sides by water

prehistoric: referring to the time before history was recorded in writing

province: a political division of a country

republic: a form of government in which the people vote their head of state into office

species: a group of living things that have common qualities

standard of living: the level of comfort people have in their lives, based on whether they can buy things they need or want

typhoons: hurricanes that occur in the western Pacific Ocean

UNESCO: the United Nations Educational, Scientific, and Cultural Organization, whose main goals are to promote world peace and eliminate poverty through education, science, and culture

urban: relating to a city or town

Index

arts 24, 25
Asia 4, 14, 15, 16, 19, 20, 22, 25, 25
automotive industry 10

baseball 26, 27
Blue House 13
border 6, 19
Buddhism 17, 18, 23, 24
Busan 15, 20, 25

Christianity 23
Confucianism 17, 18, 24
crops 9, 11, 17

demilitarization zone (DMZ) 10, 21
dynasties 17, 18, 19

economy 4, 14
electronics 14, 15

film 25

Geumg River 8
Gobi Desert 9

Han River 8, 11, 12

Incheon 20
indigenous peoples 16

Jeju Island 6, 11, 13, 22

Korean peninsula 4, 9, 16, 17, 19, 21
K-Pop 25

Lee, Jasmine 22

manufacturing 14
monsoons 9
Mount Halla 6, 13
Mount Jiri 7

Nakdong River 7, 8
North Korea 4, 6, 10, 16, 18, 21

Olympics 23, 26, 27

pagoda 12
palaces 7, 12, 13
plains 9
Pyeongchang 27

rice 11, 17

Seoul 7, 8, 12, 13, 15, 16, 18, 20, 22
shipbuilding industry 14
skiing 12, 13
Sobaek Mountains 8, 9

Taebaek Mountains 8, 9
Taekwondo 26, 27
temples 7, 12, 18, 19
typhoons 9

Yeong River 8
Yongpyong 13

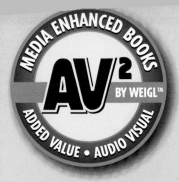

Log on to www.av2books.com

AV² by Weigl brings you media enhanced books that support active learning. Go to www.av2books.com, and enter the special code found on page 2 of this book. You will gain access to enriched and enhanced content that supplements and complements this book. Content includes video, audio, weblinks, quizzes, a slide show, and activities.

AV² Online Navigation

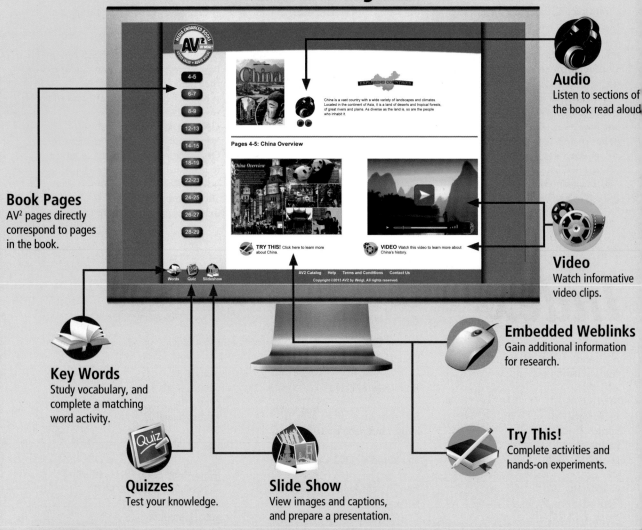

Book Pages
AV² pages directly correspond to pages in the book.

Audio
Listen to sections of the book read aloud.

Video
Watch informative video clips.

Key Words
Study vocabulary, and complete a matching word activity.

Embedded Weblinks
Gain additional information for research.

Quizzes
Test your knowledge.

Slide Show
View images and captions, and prepare a presentation.

Try This!
Complete activities and hands-on experiments.

AV² was built to bridge the gap between print and digital. We encourage you to tell us what you like and what you want to see in the future.

Sign up to be an AV² Ambassador at www.av2books.com/ambassador.

Due to the dynamic nature of the Internet, some of the URLs and activities provided as part of AV² by Weigl may have changed or ceased to exist. AV² by Weigl accepts no responsibility for any such changes. All media enhanced books are regularly monitored to update addresses and sites in a timely manner. Contact AV² by Weigl at 1-866-649-3445 or av2books@weigl.com with any questions, comments, or feedback.